BEYOND LIMITS

Exceeding Expectations & Defying Limits

JAGANNATH DULGE

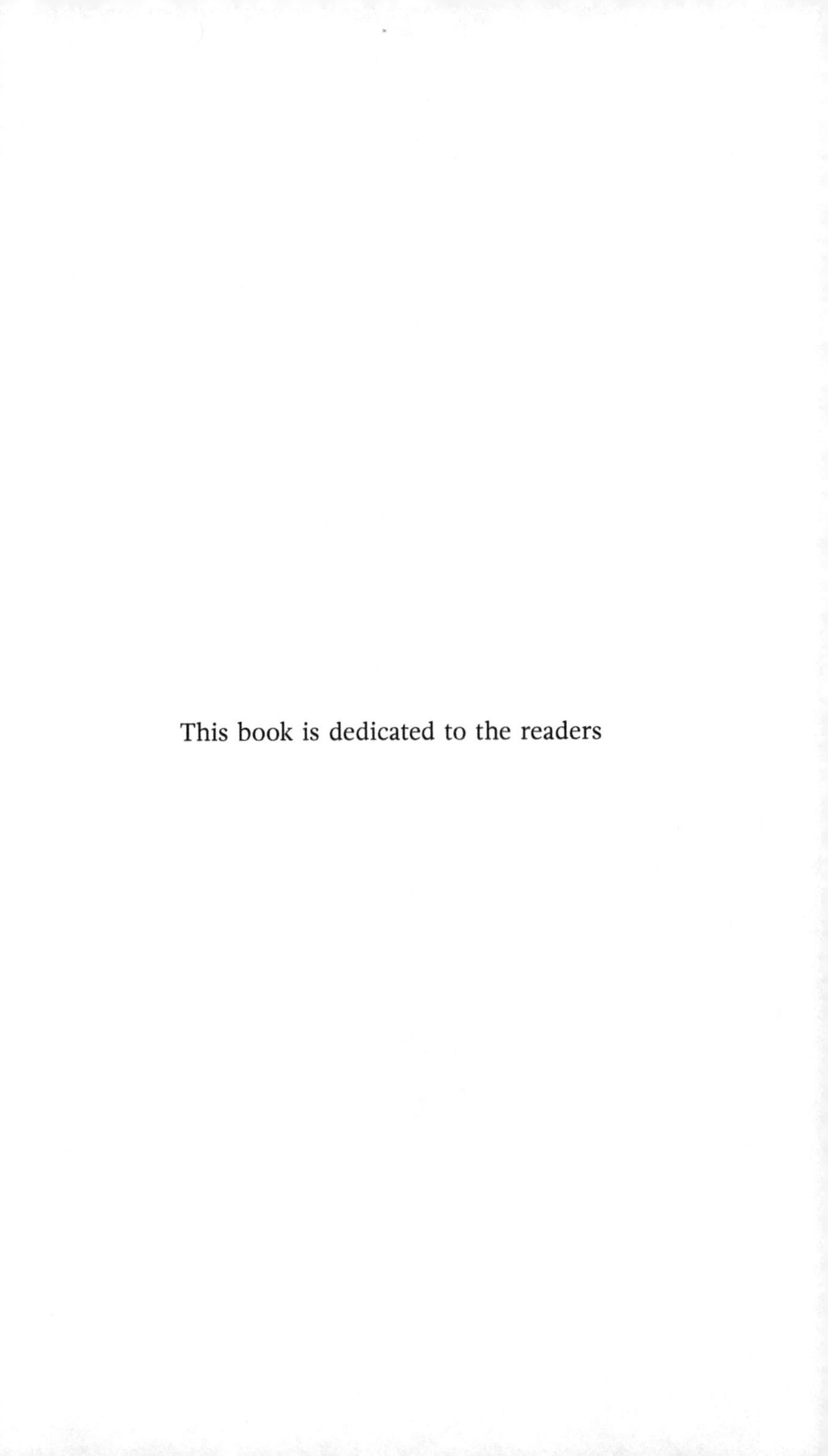

This book is dedicated to the readers

Contents

Acknowledgements

Each of us has an accumulation of unique experiences, thoughts, skills, and values woven through the loom of life. Our journey is a continuous process of learning, often through trial and error. We stumble, we fall, we rise, and in every step, we gather wisdom. This wisdom, gained through the trials and triumphs of life, is not meant to be hoarded but shared back with our society and future generations.

I feel compelled to write this book, not out of vanity or a desire for recognition, but out of a deep sense of responsibility and gratitude. Everything I have gained in this life, every lesson learned, every insight gained, belongs not just to me but to my ancestors, my society, and humanity at large. To keep this knowledge to myself would be a disservice to the world that has shaped me.

Life, with its twists and turns, has taught me invaluable lessons. Some lessons were learned the hard way, through painful mistakes and failures. Yet, in each failure, there was a seed of wisdom waiting to be nurtured. As I reflect on my journey, I realize that my experiences, both good and bad, are not just for me to keep but to share with others.

"Beyond Limits" is my attempt to give back to the world that has given me so much. It is a small token of appreciation for the lessons learned and the wisdom gained. I hope that by sharing my experiences, I can inspire others to reflect on their own journey and find meaning in their struggles.

I am deeply grateful to all those who have made this book possible. In particular, I would like to thank Dr. Mani Pavitra, my mentor and coach, whose unwavering support and encouragement have been the driving force behind this book. When I first shared the idea of writing a book, Dr. Pavitra was the first to believe in me and encouraged me to pursue my dream. Her guidance and mentorship have been invaluable, and I am forever grateful for her belief in me.

I would also like to express my gratitude to Notion Press, my publisher, for their support and assistance in bringing this book to life. Without their expertise and dedication, this book would not have reached the hands of readers. Thank you for believing in this project and helping me share my story with the world.

In writing this book, I hope to inspire others to reflect on their journey and the wisdom they have gained along the way. Life is a journey of continuous learning, and by sharing our experiences, we not only enrich our own lives but also the lives of others. Together, we can create a world where wisdom is shared, and every journey is a source of inspiration for others.

Why You Must Read This Book

In today's fast-paced and often stressful world, cultivating a positive mindset and practicing gratitude are more important than ever. Here are several compelling reasons why you should consider reading and understanding this book:

Improved Mental Health: Studies have shown that positive thinking and gratitude can significantly improve mental health by reducing symptoms of anxiety and depression. Reading books on these topics can provide you with strategies and insights to enhance your well-being.

Enhanced Resilience: Positive thinking and gratitude can help build resilience, enabling you to bounce back more easily from setbacks and challenges. Understanding these concepts can empower you to navigate life's ups and downs with greater strength and optimism.

Better Relationships: A positive attitude and a grateful mindset can improve your relationships with others. By reading books on these subjects, you can learn how to cultivate empathy, understanding, and appreciation in your interactions with others.

4. Increased Happiness: Positive thinking and gratitude are closely linked to increased feelings of happiness and satisfaction with life. By learning more about these concepts, you can discover how to cultivate greater happiness in your own life.

5. Health Benefits: Research has shown that positive thinking and gratitude can have physical health benefits, such as reduced stress levels and improved cardiovascular health. Understanding these concepts through reading can motivate you to incorporate them into your daily life.

6. Enhanced Problem-Solving Skills: A positive mindset can enhance your problem-solving skills by enabling you to approach challenges with a more open and creative mindset. Books on positive thinking can provide you with practical strategies for applying this approach in your life.

7. Increased Success: Positive thinking and gratitude are associated with increased success in various areas of life, including work, relationships, and personal goals. By reading books on these topics, you can learn how to harness these forces to achieve greater success in your own life.

8. Stress Reduction: Positive thinking and gratitude can help reduce stress levels by promoting a more optimistic and resilient mindset. Reading books on these subjects can provide you with techniques for managing stress more effectively.

Reading and understanding principles in this book on positive thinking and an attitude of gratitude can have a profound impact on your life, leading to improved mental health, enhanced resilience, better relationships, increased happiness, and numerous other benefits. Consider incorporating these books into your reading list to discover the transformative power of these concepts.

Author Profile

Jagannath Dulge, a seasoned Personality Development Trainer with over two decades of experience, specialized in Soft Skills and Sales Training. Having trained 50,000+ participants across diverse industries, his impact is evident at various organizational levels.

In academia, Mr. Dulge serves as a visiting faculty, enriching educational institutes. Corporates seek his expertise for tailored training, a testament to his versatile skill set.

Driven by a passion for results, Dulge believes in continuous self-improvement as the key to personal and professional success.

As the visionary founder of Maxam Mind (www.maxammind.com), a distinguished corporate training firm, Dulge champions continuous education. Maxam Mind's mission is clear: empower human resources through impactful learning experiences. Dulge's training footprint extends to Tata Steel, Coca-Cola, Accenture, HDFC, HPCL, Canon, Cholamandalam Insurance, Flipkart, and others, reflecting his influence in both the public and private sectors.

In addition to his extensive industry experience, Mr. Dulge has actively contributed to academia as a visiting faculty member in several esteemed educational institutes. His expertise has been sought after by numerous corporate entities, where he has been empanelled to address a myriad of training requirements.

AUTHOR PROFILE

Highlights Of The Book

In the realm of personal development, two universal principles stand out for their profound impact on human life: positive thinking and gratitude. Understanding and implementing these principles can indeed change the course of our lives, transforming every area from our relationships to our career paths.

Positive thinking is not merely about wearing a smile or suppressing negative emotions. It's a mindset that focuses on finding the good in every situation. This approach helps us maintain optimism and resilience in the face of challenges, fostering a proactive attitude toward problem-solving. By consciously directing our thoughts towards positive outcomes, we can reshape our reality and attract more favourable circumstances.

Similarly, gratitude is a potent force that can shift our perspective from scarcity to abundance. When we cultivate gratitude, we acknowledge and appreciate the blessings, big and small, in our lives. This practice not only enhances our overall sense of well-being but also attracts more positive experiences. By recognizing and being thankful for what we have, we invite more reasons to be grateful into our lives.

Implementing these powers requires consistent practice and mindfulness. Start by reframing negative thoughts into positive affirmations. Instead of dwelling on what's lacking, focus on what you're grateful for

By integrating positive thinking and gratitude into our daily lives, we can witness a profound transformation. Our relationships become more harmonious, our work more fulfilling, and our overall outlook more optimistic. These principles are not mere platitudes but potent tools that can truly change the fabric of our existence.

Positive thinking and gratitude are not just abstract concepts; they are actionable strategies that can enhance our lives in unimaginable ways. These principles have changed the lives of millions. It is your turn to harness the power of these two forces so, we can steer our lives towards greater happiness, success, and fulfillment.

Chapter 1: The Impact of Positive Thinking on Success

"Inspiration comes from within yourself. One has to be positive. When you're positive, good things happen." —Deep Roy

Positive thinking is not just a fleeting feeling of happiness or optimism; it's a mindset that can profoundly impact our lives and success. At its core, positive thinking is the practice of focusing on the good in any given situation and expecting positive outcomes. This approach can significantly influence our mental and physical well-being, as well as our ability to achieve our goals.

What Is Positive Thinking?

Positive thinking is a mental attitude that anticipates favorable outcomes and expects good results. It involves focusing on the positive aspects of a situation rather than dwelling on the negatives. This mindset is not about ignoring problems or challenges; instead, it's about approaching them with a constructive and optimistic outlook.

Positive thinking is rooted in the belief that our thoughts shape our reality. By maintaining positive thoughts, we can attract positive outcomes and experiences into our lives. This mindset is often associated with concepts like the law of attraction, which suggests that positive or negative thoughts can bring positive or negative experiences, respectively.

The Impact of Positive Thinking on Success

1. Improved Mental Health: Positive thinking can have a significant impact on mental health. It can reduce stress, anxiety, and depression, leading to a more balanced and resilient mindset. By focusing on positive thoughts, individuals can improve their overall well-being and emotional stability.

Positive thinking acts as a beacon of light in the realm of mental health, illuminating pathways to resilience and well-being. Its impact resonates deeply, touching every aspect of our mental landscape and fostering a sense of optimism and hope. One of the key benefits of positive thinking is its ability to reduce stress and anxiety. Just as the ripples on the lake gradually calm the waters, positive thoughts can soothe the mind and ease feelings of tension and worry. This can lead to improved mental clarity and a greater sense of peace.

Positive thinking also plays a crucial role in building resilience. Like a sturdy boat that navigates the waters of life, a resilient mind can weather the storms of adversity with grace and strength. By fostering a positive outlook, individuals can cultivate resilience and bounce back from challenges more effectively. Furthermore, positive thinking can enhance self-esteem and self-confidence. Just as the ripples on the lake reflect the beauty of the surrounding landscape, positive thoughts can reflect our inherent worth and value. This can lead to a greater sense of self-assurance and belief in one's abilities.

The impact of positive thinking on mental health is profound and far-reaching. By nurturing optimism, we can create a ripple effect of positivity that transforms our mental landscape, fostering resilience, reducing stress, and enhancing our overall well-being.

2. Enhanced Physical Health: Research has shown that positive thinking can also benefit physical health. Positive individuals tend to have lower levels of stress hormones, which can reduce the risk of various health issues, including cardiovascular diseases and chronic illnesses. Positive thinking serves as a bridge between the mind and the body, facilitating a profound impact on physical health. Just as a river flows effortlessly, positive thoughts can enhance the body's natural healing processes and promote overall well-being. Positive thinking has been linked to a range of physical health benefits, including lower stress levels, reduced risk of cardiovascular diseases, and improved immune function. When we think positively, our bodies release hormones that promote relaxation and reduce stress, which can have a direct impact on our physical health.

3. Increased Resilience: Positive thinking fosters resilience, allowing individuals to bounce back from setbacks and challenges more effectively. This resilience is crucial for success, as it enables individuals to persevere in the face of adversity.

Positive thinking acts as a bedrock of resilience, shaping our ability to navigate life's challenges with grace and determination. Like a sturdy foundation, positive thoughts lay the groundwork for resilience, enabling us to bounce back from adversity and emerge stronger than before.

When we approach difficult situations with a positive mindset, we are better able to see setbacks as temporary and setbacks as opportunities for growth. This optimistic outlook fuels our resilience, motivating us to persevere in the face of adversity and overcome obstacles with confidence.

4. Improved Relationships: Positive thinking can also improve relationships. Optimistic individuals are more likely to approach interactions with empathy, understanding, and positivity, leading to stronger and more fulfilling relationships.

Positive thinking catalyzes fostering strong and meaningful relationships. When individuals approach interactions with a positive mindset, they are more likely to communicate effectively, show empathy, and build trust with others. Positive thinking can also enhance our ability to resolve conflicts constructively. Instead of focusing on blame or criticism, individuals who think positively are more likely to seek mutually beneficial solutions and maintain respect for each other's perspectives.

It can create a positive feedback loop in relationships, where acts of kindness and positivity are reciprocated, leading to deeper connections and a stronger bond.

5. Enhanced Problem-Solving Skills: Positive thinking is associated with enhanced problem-solving skills. By focusing on solutions rather than problems, individuals can approach challenges more effectively and find creative solutions.

Positive thinking serves as a stimulus for effective problem-solving, empowering individuals to approach challenges with optimism. When faced with a problem, those who think positively are more likely to see it as a solvable challenge rather than an insurmountable obstacle.

Positive thinking enhances our ability to think creatively and explore innovative solutions. By maintaining a positive outlook, individuals can overcome mental barriers and think outside the box, leading to more effective problem-solving strategies. It enables confidence and motivation, encouraging individuals to persevere in the face of setbacks. This resilience is crucial for problem-solving, as it allows individuals to stay focused and determined until a solution is found.

6. Boosted Confidence: Positive thinking can boost confidence and self-esteem. When individuals believe in themselves and their abilities, they are more likely to take risks and pursue their goals with determination.

Positive thinking is the main ingredient of confidence, empowering individuals to believe in their abilities and pursue their goals with conviction. When we think positively, we cultivate a mindset of self-assurance and optimism that can propel us to new heights of achievement.

Positive thinking enhances our self-image and self-esteem, helping us to view ourselves in a more positive light. This, in turn, boosts our confidence and belief in our capabilities, enabling us to take on new challenges with courage and determination.

Furthermore, positive thinking can help us overcome self-doubt and fear of failure, two common barriers to confidence. By focusing on positive outcomes and possibilities, we can build the confidence needed to step out of our comfort zones and embrace new opportunities.

7. Increased Success: Ultimately, positive thinking can lead to greater success in various aspects of life. Whether in personal relationships, career endeavors, or personal development, maintaining a positive mindset can open doors to opportunities and help individuals achieve their goals.

Positive thinking serves as a driving force behind success, shaping our attitudes and actions in ways that propel us toward our goals. When we maintain optimism, we approach challenges with a can-do attitude, viewing them as opportunities for growth rather than obstacles.

Positive thinking also enhances our resilience, enabling us to bounce back from setbacks and persevere in the face of adversity. This resilience is crucial for success, as it allows us to stay focused and determined even when faced with obstacles.

Strategies for Cultivating Positive Thinking

1. Stay away from negative social media: The media we consume has a profound effect on our mental and emotional well-being. While tragic movies and books can evoke strong emotions, they can also leave us feeling drained and despondent. To cultivate a more positive mindset, it's essential to be mindful of the content we engage with.

Instead of watching tragic movies, negative news on social media, print media, or reading books that focus on negativity, consider opting for inspirational movies, podcasts, and videos. These forms of media can uplift and motivate us, inspiring a more optimistic outlook on life. They can also provide valuable lessons and insights that empower us to overcome challenges and strive for personal growth. By making a conscious choice to surround ourselves with positive influences, we can enhance our mental and emotional resilience, leading to a more fulfilling and rewarding life.

2. Challenge Negative Thoughts: Negative thoughts can cloud our minds and dampen our spirits, but they don't have to control us. When negative thoughts arise, we have the power to challenge them and shift our perspective. This simple yet powerful practice can help us reframe our mindset and outlook, leading to greater positivity and resilience.

One effective way to challenge negative thoughts is through positive affirmations. By repeating positive statements about ourselves and our abilities, we can counteract the negativity and build self-confidence. Another approach is to seek alternative perspectives. Instead of automatically accepting negative thoughts as truth, we can consider alternative explanations or interpretations that are more positive and empowering. By challenging negative thoughts, we can take control of our minds and cultivate a more optimistic and resilient outlook on life.

3. Surround Yourself with Positivity: Our surroundings have a profound impact on our mind and well-being. To cultivate a positive outlook on life, it's essential to surround ourselves with positivity in all aspects of our lives. One way to surround yourself with positivity is through uplifting books that inspire and motivate you. Reading stories of triumph over adversity or self-help books can uplift your spirits and encourage personal growth.

Another way to create a positive environment is by surrounding yourself with supportive friends and loved ones who uplift and encourage you. Their positivity can be contagious, uplifting your spirits and reinforcing a positive mindset. Finally, consider your physical environment. Create a space that inspires you, whether it's through uplifting artwork, soothing colours, or a clutter-free environment. By intentionally surrounding yourself with positivity, you can cultivate a mindset that is resilient, optimistic, and ready to take on life's challenges.

4. Visualize Success: Visualization is a powerful tool that can help us achieve our goals and maintain a positive mindset. By imagining ourselves succeeding and achieving our dreams, we can boost our motivation and reinforce a positive outlook on life.

When we visualize success, we create a mental image of our desired outcome. This image acts as a powerful motivator, inspiring us to take action and work towards our goals. Additionally, visualization can help us overcome self-doubt and fear of failure, as we focus on the positive outcomes we want to achieve.

To harness the power of visualization, find a quiet space where you can relax and focus. Close your eyes and imagine yourself achieving your goals in vivid detail. Visualize how you will feel, what you will see, and what steps you will take to reach your goals.

By incorporating visualization into your daily routine, you can cultivate a positive mindset and propel yourself towards success.

5. Practice Mindfulness: Mindfulness is a powerful practice that can transform the way we think and act. By focusing and staying conscious about natural breathing we can choose to be calm over impulsive reactions.

Mindfulness teaches us to observe our breath without judgment, allowing us to become more aware of natural breath. This awareness gives us the power to choose how we respond to situations, rather than reacting automatically. When we practice mindfulness, we become more in tune with our emotions and can better regulate them. This can lead to improved relationships and a greater sense of inner peace.

To incorporate mindfulness into your daily life, take time to pause and breathe deeply. Focus on the present moment, letting go of worries about the past or future. With practice, mindfulness can become a powerful tool for cultivating positivity and resilience in all areas of your life.

6. Practice affirmations: Affirmations are powerful statements that can help rewire our thoughts and beliefs, leading to a more positive mindset and increased self-confidence. By practicing affirmations regularly, we can cultivate a mindset of success and resilience.

To practice affirmations, choose statements that resonate with you and reflect the positive qualities you want to embody. Repeat these affirmations daily, either silently or out loud, and visualize yourself living out these truths.

- Affirmation 1: "I am becoming better and better day by day".
- Affirmation 2: "Every day and every way I am becoming more and more positive".
- Affirmation 3: "I am attracting abundance in my life".
- Affirmation 4: "I am improving my physical and mental health better and better day by day".
- Affirmation 5: "I am becoming more and more successful in my life day by day".

Affirmations can help challenge and overcome negative self-talk, replacing it with empowering beliefs. They can also boost motivation and reinforce a positive outlook on life. By incorporating affirmations into your daily routine, you can transform your mindset and unlock your full potential for success and happiness.

Positive thinking is a powerful tool that can transform our lives and lead to greater success and fulfillment. By cultivating a positive mindset, we can improve our mental and physical health, enhance our relationships, and increase our chances of achieving our goals. It's important to remember that positive thinking is not about denying reality or ignoring challenges but rather approaching them with optimism, resilience, and a proactive attitude. Embracing positive thinking can truly be a game-changer in our quest for success and happiness.

"Only in the darkness you can see the stars." —Martin Luther King, Jr.

I ask sometimes my students. What were your best days of life? Most of them would say, college days. What about you? For me, the worst days of my life were my college days. I did not enjoy my college days. I wanted to study seriously. I wanted to learn and grow. I used to think what we study and learn in college that would have a huge impact on our future, career, and life. I was damn serious about it. For me, college was building your future in the present moment. But the rest of the students and probably professors too. For them, college life is a time pass. Fun time. Party time. Hanging out with girls or friends. College means entertainment. Most of the students used to go mass bunking for them it was fun. Bunking lectures for me was offensive. For other students spending time in the canteen was fun. For me reading books, studying, or spending time in the library was fun and entertainment. Sometimes lecturers were not coming due to mass bunking. Somehow lectures were not happening as regularly as they were supposed to. For me, it was not acceptable. I felt restlessness. I was right at the right place but the environment was not supportive. Nothing was working in my favour. It was boring for me. I lost interest in studying and in college. So I got into depression. I stopped enjoying my college days. life in college days.

In the beginning, I was not aware of what was happening. It continued for 2-3 years. Some of my relatives started recommending do this, do that. I tried all. Still did not have the remedy. One of my relatives suggested me a visiting Psychiatrist from Hyderabad. I consulted him. He prescribed me some medicine. I followed his instructions for 2-3 months. But no relief.

I moved to Mumbai in search of a job. I spent a couple of months in Mumbai in search of a job. I did not know how to prepare a resume for a job to send the companies and how to dress and groom for the job interview. Where to find a job or how to find a job was all this mystery for me. Forget about cracking interviews in the English language.

I have trained thousands of students on interview preparation, dressing, and grooming for interviews and conducted many mock interviews of interviews. Once I was suffering from interview phobia. Now after my training and guidance, many students were able to crack job interviews in the first attempt.

But being a mechanical engineer I had no clue how to get a job. I did not have a guide or mentor to show me the right path to walk. Now I think most of the graduates face the same problem. When I see the college final year students or freshers I recall my nightmares.

My situation was getting worse. I did not have money to eat or spend too. I was mentally unstable. I did know how to ask for a job too. Life was merciless. After a lot of struggles and hardships for several months could not find a job or internship for me. I did not have enough money to buy a bus ticket to go back to my hometown. I worked as a daily wage construction labourer for some days earned my expenses and came back to my hometown.

One fine day I saw a classified ad for some sales executives in Hyderabad. I appeared for the interview, I was clueless about how companies operated and how they looked. The interviewer committed to me a lot of salary, increments, incentives, promotions, and bonuses. Later stage, I came to know that he was a con man. It was his trap to cheat young and fresh job seekers who come to cities in search of jobs.

I found a credit card selling agency later and joined the agency. While working in the agency I rented a room and continued working.

"There is a way on the way – Unknown

One day, when I was going through the local newspaper, saw a classified ad that caught my eyesight. This classified was about a Counselor cum Hypnotherapist, who had remedies for depression and anxiety. I did not know anything about counseling or hypnotherapy. However, I was more interested in the word depression and anxiety. I was curious. I wanted to check, what is the matter. One day I approached the counselor and tried to understand what it was all about this and does he had any cure for my depression. He confirmed that it would be charged per session. He realized that I could not afford his charges. He took whatever I had and asked me to pay me later. He told me to visit twice in week for therapy sittings for two months. I accepted his offer.

I took his sessions at the concession price. Along with these therapy sessions he suggested some books to read. The books were Unlimited Power and Awaken the Giant Within by Anthony Robbins.

I went to the bookstore, I found the books and checked the prices. Those books were unaffordable for me. I could not afford those two books. Instead of buying those two books, I bought a cheaper book on the same subject.

Along with therapy sittings, I started reading The Silva Mind Control and Sales Power by Jose Silva. This book had two important lessons that I needed the most as I was selling credit cards and I was depressed. This book was about selling skills as well as human psychology.

Within two months of counseling therapy sessions and lessons, I learned and practiced by reading this book. Both helped me to overcome my mental depression. I started feeling lighter, happier, and full of self-confidence.

The Silva Mind Control Method helped me to think positively in life. This book had some practical daily assignments to complete for the readers. I followed all the instructions in the book. And completed all the assignments on time. This book made me realize What is positive thinking and what are advantages of positive thinking. I learned and started practicing positive thinking.

Once I overcame this depression, I never went back. This positive thinking helped me to stay positive throughout my life.

Activity: Write all the positive things that happened in the day for the next 21 days at

the end of every day. It takes around 21 days to build any habit. By making a list for 21 days, you can develop a habit of positive thinking within 21 days. Then you can continue for life as long as you wish to have positive thinking in life.

Chapter 2: The Power of Gratitude

"Gratitude is one of the strongest and most transformative states of being. It shifts your perspective from lack to abundance and allows you to focus on the good in your life, which in turn pulls more goodness into your reality." — Jen Sincero

Gratitude, a sentiment often exchanged casually, unveils a profound emotional symphony when explored through the lens of science. It's not just a courtesy; it's a transformative force that touches the depths of our emotions.

At its core lies the impact on mental well-being. Delving into gratitude is akin to opening the floodgates of positive emotions. Neurotransmitters like dopamine and serotonin, the architects of joy, flood our minds with a warmth that transcends mere words. It's a poignant dance of chemicals, a melody that soothes the soul.

Imagine gratitude as a balm for the heart, a remedy that heals wounds we might not even realize we carry. Scientific studies reveal that actively practicing gratitude leads to lower levels of stress and depression, offering solace to the emotional landscape.

Yet, it's more than a coping mechanism; it's a guiding light through life's trials. Gratitude isn't about denying challenges but embracing a perspective that finds beauty in adversity. It's a lifeline that pulls us through stormy emotional seas.

Adding a touch of emotional nuance, gratitude emerges as a silent hero in the story of our emotions. It's the friend who understands our unspoken pain, bringing comfort like a familiar melody in times of sorrow. In a world filled with complexities, gratitude becomes a gentle whisper amid the chaos, a reminder that even in darkness, there is light.

Envision the heart, adorned with the crown of gratitude, navigating the emotional landscape with grace. It's more than a choice; it's an emotional declaration—a testament to resilience and an embrace of the spectrum of human feelings.

In conclusion, the science behind gratitude is a journey into the heart's terrain. As you tread this path, remember that gratitude isn't just a mental exercise; it's an emotional revelation. May your days be graced with moments that evoke a profound "thank you" from the depths of your heart.

In the intricate tapestry of human emotions, gratitude stands out as a thread that weaves joy into the fabric of our lives. Beyond mere pleasantries, expressing gratitude is akin to unlocking a treasure trove of psychological benefits that science now illuminates.

At the forefront is the profound impact on mental health. When we consciously cultivate gratitude, our brains undergo a fascinating transformation. Neurotransmitters like dopamine and serotonin, often hailed as the brain's 'feel-good' chemicals, surge in response to expressions of thanks. It's not just a fleeting emotion; it's a biochemical symphony that tunes our minds to a positive frequency.

Imagine gratitude as a mental gym, where the workout involves lifting the weights of appreciation. Studies have shown that individuals who regularly engage in gratitude exercises exhibit lower levels of stress and depression. It's not a magic potion but a scientifically-backed elixir for a resilient mind.

"Gratitude can transform common days into thanksgivings, turn routine jobs into joy, and change ordinary opportunities into blessings." - William Arthur Ward

In my family and my community, I was the brightest child. I was a school topper in high school. Everyone thought I would make great in my life.

It was time I was completely broke financially and professionally. I was earning hand-to-mouth. I was working as a freelancer soft skills trainer. I never had more than 15 days of work in a month. Once the family was admiring and proud of me. Started taking me lightly. Jagannath used to be smart in his academics and no more. He is bright and smart; he has a lot of knowledge but no use. All the knowledge, and skills of Jagannath are useless and worthless. Many of his friends were dumb but doing far better than Jagannath. My family and relatives started disrespecting and ignoring me. Their behavior annoyed me a lot. I was hurt deeply. But helpless and clueless. Sometimes I wondered what is the problem with me.

For me, it was hurting. It was painful. First time in my life I was worried about my life and career. I was asking myself again and again. Is it my life? Is it worth living? My future was looking me dark. I started doubting myself and my ability. Is it the dead end of my life?

I was living a pretty average life. It was boring meaningless and directionless.

One day, my wife's colleague forced my wife to buy the book The Magic written by Rhonda Berne. My wife brought it and kept it at home on the table. I hope she did not even bother to see that book.

I took it. Started reading The Magic. I kept on reading the first four chapters. Within the short duration, I had a training assignment in a different city for a month.

It had a series of activities to complete over 28 days. I was very excited to read and complete those activities as per the author's instructions. I was reading each topic twice a day and making a list of 10 blessings of my life. I did it every day for 28 days without missing a single day.

By now I was good at practicing gratitude. I had developed the habit of gratitude. Then suddenly many miracles started happening in my life. I started getting more work gradually. I started earning more than enough. I started saving a little amount of whatever I could.

I knew many forms of meditation and breathing techniques but did not practice them.

One day suddenly decided to start pranayama (breathing technique). Gradually I build a habit of my own. I combined both the practice of gratitude and pranayama.

After a couple of months started meditation as well. I practiced meditation one day. Days became weeks and weeks became months.

Within a short duration, I imbibed the practice of gratitude, pranayama, and meditation.

Once I started practicing these three I started feeling more relaxed, calm, composed, light and energetic. I was getting more days of work and earning more pay.

My new journey of abundance began. Many good and great things started happening in my life. Gradually I began to attract more training assignments. Some through training consultancies, some directly from educational institutes, and some from corporates. I was earning more now. At least better than before. Started saving some money. I was attracting more beautiful and magical moments. From every area of life started attracting positive things and good things. Sometimes personal, sometimes professional, sometimes financial, sometimes relationship, and sometimes emotional. I was on cloud nine. I was enjoying the process of counting my blessings every day. My work had become my love. Feeling happy doing little things in a great way. I could see riches and abundance in every area of my life.

Activity: Write a gratitude journal for the next 21 days, noting seven things you're thankful for each day.

Chapter 3: Overcoming Adversity with Resilience

"If you run into a wall, don't turn around and give up. Figure out how to climb it."
– Michael Jordan

Life is a journey filled with ups and downs, challenges and triumphs. In the face of adversity, our ability to overcome obstacles and emerge stronger is often determined by our mindset. Positive thinking and gratitude play crucial roles in cultivating resilience, helping us navigate tough times with grace and strength.

Positive thinking is more than just a sunny outlook; it's a mindset that focuses on solutions rather than problems. When we approach challenges with a positive attitude, we are better equipped to find creative solutions and persevere in the face of adversity. This mindset shift can significantly impact how we experience and respond to difficult situations.

Gratitude, too, plays a pivotal role in building resilience. By focusing on the things we are thankful for, even amid adversity, we can shift our perspective and find moments of joy and peace. Gratitude reminds us of the good in our lives, even when times are tough, and can help us maintain a positive outlook.

Together, positive thinking and gratitude create a powerful combination that can help us overcome adversity with resilience. Here's how:

1. **Positive Thinking Helps Reframe Challenges:** When faced with adversity, it's easy to feel overwhelmed and defeated. However, positive thinking can help reframe these challenges as opportunities for growth and learning. Instead of focusing on the negatives, we can look for silver linings and ways to turn the situation around.

2. **Gratitude Cultivates Resilience:** Practicing gratitude in difficult times helps us focus on the positives in our lives, no matter how small. This can help shift our mindset from one of despair to one of hope and resilience. By acknowledging the good, we can find the strength to keep moving forward.

3. **They Promote Emotional Well-being:** Positive thinking and gratitude can have a profound impact on our emotional well-being. They help reduce stress, anxiety, and depression, all of which can hinder our ability to cope with adversity. By maintaining a positive mindset and practicing gratitude, we can improve our mental health and resilience.

4. **They Foster a Supportive Mindset:** Positive thinking and gratitude also help foster a

mindset of support and collaboration. Instead of viewing others as competitors or obstacles, we see them as potential allies and resources. This mindset shift can help us build a strong support network, which is crucial for overcoming adversity.

5. **They Enhance Problem-Solving Skills:** Positive thinking and gratitude can also enhance our problem-solving skills. Instead of getting stuck in a cycle of negative thinking, we are more likely to approach problems with a clear and focused mind. This can lead to more effective solutions and a quicker resolution of challenges.

Positive thinking and gratitude are powerful tools that can help us overcome adversity with resilience. By cultivating these qualities, we can shift our mindset, improve our emotional well-being, and enhance our problem-solving skills. In doing so, we can navigate life's challenges with grace and emerge stronger and more resilient than ever before.

"Strength does not come from winning. Your struggles develop your strengths. When you go through hardships and decide not to surrender, that is strength." - Arnold Schwarzenegger

My wife and I decided to buy a house. I started searching nearby areas. By the way, we did not have enough payment for the down payment. We had some savings but it was not enough.

After seeing so many ready and under-construction projects, one day we both finalized an apartment in an under-construction project. We did not have a full down payment as well we did not have faith that we would get a home loan too. Even some financial institutions fund but whether we could repay loan EMI's at least for a year. Somehow we earned and paid a down payment and we got financed. It has been more than 8 years. Touch would we haven't even missed an EMI.

I was leading a calm, cool, and peaceful life. I had my own house. I was leading a content life with whatever I had. I was doing better than earlier personally, professionally, and financially. This was all happening because of the practice of gratitude, meditation, and pranayama.

In 2016 one day my wife met with an accident. She was hurt badly. It was painful. We met many specialists. They asked to do X-rays, scanning of the knee, and an MRI test. We had discussions with specialists in Orthopedic Surgeons. Eventually, Ortho-surgeons recommended us to go through ACL surgery. Implantation had to be done in the knee. The hospital gave us an estimation of Rs.1,00,000/- Arranging Rs. 1,00,000/- was not that easy for us, but we had to arrange it. After having a lot of discussions we as a family decided to go for surgery.

We did not have a medical claim insurance policy, so I had to arrange my own. I managed the amount on my own. The day of surgery came. Ortho-surgeon operated the surgery. It was painful. My wife Neelaveni had gone through hell. We did not have a better choice. We had to go through it eventually. We all just hoped everything would be alright. The hospital discharged us after the 2-3 days of surgery and asked us to visit the hospital for a regular checkup.

After a few days of surgery, my wife Neelaveni was crying due to heavy pain in her knee. We rushed to the hospital, for a check-up. The surgeon checked her, prescribed her some medicines, and asked her to take complete rest. Neelaveni was in severe pain but she had to suffer.

After a couple of weeks, visited the surgeon again. This time the surgeon suggested doing an X-ray, scanning, and MRI as well to know the current status of the knee implantation. The specialist found be infection in the knee where the knee was operated. Her body could not accept the external object as an implant. The hospital recommended the removal of the implant from the knee otherwise it would spread in the body and it could be dangerous too. The priority was to remove the infection and let it heal the surgery. After complete healing of the pain, they could implant again. We were in shock. We could not believe this would happen. We thought the surgery would end the problem. It was leading more.

We came back home. We tried to take 2nd opinion. We tried 3rd and more opinions. Almost all surgeons and orthopedics recommended the same thing. Priority basis we had to remove the implant from the knee before it is too late.

The pain was unbearable for my wife. She did not want to go for another surgery but in the fear of infection spreading, she agreed. Finance part I had to manage. The money was not ready. I needed to arrange it. This time it was costing me Rs.1,50, 000/-

My best friend Raghavendra Hosamani took his credit card from his wallet and kept it in my pocket without asking me a single word. I cannot forget that gesture in my life. It is a blessing to have such timely friends.

The second surgery was not easy. My wife cried and suffered a lot due to this. She was traumatized badly. Sometimes pain was unbearable. I could not see her crying and suffering. I was seeing this with my own eyes suffering her silently. It took almost 1-2 years to cure this infection in the knee.

After these two surgeries one for implantation in the knee and the second for removal of the implantation causing infection, my wife said no to another surgery for implantation.

Throughout this incident, I was observing my thought process and emotional, and mental status, the incident was painful, it traumatized my soulmate emotionally, mentally, and physically, but I was calm, patient, and composed. I was emotionally and mentally balanced. Because I was regularly practicing gratitude, meditation, and pranayama every day. This incident did not hinder me. It could not traumatize me. Because of this continuous and consistent practice, I had enough strength to sail the terrible event smoothly.

You know what else happened? I was doing better than ever before in my career. I started my new branch of the Maxam Mind Personality Development Institute same year. It was growing rapidly. Students started to walk in more and more day by day. I was growing financially. I was paying my Home loan EMIs. I was getting more training assignments. I earned and paid my wife's bills of Rs.1,50,000/- She had gone for physiotherapy for almost more than a year. Despite my hardships, I managed my institute, my finances, and my freelance assignments without panicking. I was enjoying my work and my growth. All credit goes to my attitude of gratitude, the regular 1-hour practice of meditation, and pranayama. Daily 1 hour of this practice gave me energy, good health, and emotional and mental strength to manage my whole life effortlessly. I regained my self-confidence, my finances, my career, and my identity.

Activity: Practice positive affirmations daily for two weeks and note any changes in mood or perspective.

Chapter 4: Manifesting through Intention and Focus

**"Every intention sets energy into motion, whether you are aware of it or not."
- Henry David Thoreau**

Manifestation is the process of turning your thoughts and desires into reality through intention and focus. By combining the power of positive thinking and gratitude with intentional focus, you can manifest your dreams and create the life you desire.

Positive thinking is essential for manifestation, as it helps to align your thoughts and beliefs with your goals. When you maintain a positive mindset, you are more likely to attract positive outcomes and opportunities into your life. Gratitude also plays a crucial role, as it helps to amplify positive emotions and attract more of what you are thankful for.

Intention is the key to manifestation, as it sets the direction for your thoughts and actions. By setting clear intentions for what you want to manifest, you can focus your energy and attention on achieving your goals. Focus is also important, as it helps you to stay committed to your intentions and take the necessary steps to bring them to fruition.

To manifest your dreams, start by identifying what you want to achieve or attract into your life. Then, create a clear intention statement that reflects your goals and desires. Use positive affirmations and visualization techniques to reinforce your intentions and stay focused on your goals. Practice gratitude daily, focusing on all the things you are thankful for in your life.

As you continue to focus on your intentions and maintain a positive mindset, you will begin to see your dreams manifesting in your life. Remember to stay open to receiving and trust in the process. With the support of positive thinking, gratitude, intention, and focus, you can manifest your dreams and create the life you desire.

"When you want something from the bottom of your heart, the entire universe conspires to achieve it."
- Paulo Coelho

Recent past I had a teacher training assignment with the Naval School at Uran Navi Mumbai. There were around 20 teachers in the session. I had 1-2 sessions in a week. The teachers were very passionate about learning as well as teaching the school students. I was very fortunate to take sessions with such wonderful teachers.

My sessions were mostly interactive, practical, and result-oriented. We had usually many activities, games, role plays, stories, group discussions, debates, and assessments in our sessions.

It was November month 2018. One day, one of the participants Chandrika Jadhav shared a story. It was her story of childhood to adulthood. She was very close to her mother in her childhood more than her father. Mother was spending more time with her. Whatever she needed, she was asking her mother only. If she had any good moments or bad moments, everything she would share with her mother only. Her mother was her best friend throughout her life.

She was just average in her studies in her entire academics. She never participated in any school contests or competitions. So never tasted the taste of success in her whole academics.

Chandrika narrated the biggest regret of her in her own words. Her father would look at her and he would always think when would his daughter go on stage bring trophies and victories for him and make him proud. He was disappointed with his daughter's performance. He was expecting some excellence in her studies. Due to this, he was never able to develop a good rapport with her. He was not too resentful or regretful towards her also but he had an unfulfilled wish to see his daughter go on stage and receive a reward or prize on the stage.

Meanwhile, she completed her graduation and post-graduation with her B. Ed. and became an English school teacher. She got married and had a cute and smart son. Somehow father and daughter became very close and now they enjoy their time together with her son.

Still she had had a regret in her life till that time, that she could not fulfil her father's wish. This was bothering her for a long time.

Even though she is a teacher and teaches so many students and makes a difference in many students' and parents' lives. However, she was not able to go back and create proud moments in her life for her father. She would say "I wish; I could." She had a burning desire to do something: undo or redo for her father.

However, Day by day it had become an obsession with this wish. She had this life's biggest wish to be fulfilled her father's wish. At this juncture in life, she was not able to do anything to make her father's wish. But she had a deep and strong desire to make it happen. She was ready to do anything and everything to make it happen. She shared this story in deep frustration. It used to pain her a lot. But she was helpless.

As usual, I continued sessions for a couple of months. One day she called me on my personal cell phone number, I was in the middle of a session and told her that I would call her back after the session. I called her after the session, she was so happy and excited in her voice. She asked me " I need your help, Sir?" I said. What help, do you need?

"Sir, I got an invitation from my childhood school. The school principal Sir had invited me for facilitation of me as a successful student of the school. They are going to facilitate me on the school's annual day and school management asked me to give a short speech on that day." She needed my help in preparing the speech for the day.

She was overwhelmed by this news because she was going to be called on the stage and this all going to happen in front of her father. This was her father's wish and this was the moment to make her father proud.

The facilitation day came and over. The next day, she narrated the entire incident in front of her colleagues and me in the session. She had gone to school with her parents, brother, husband, and 3-year-old son. Her family was seated in the front row. Her brother was video shooting the event. She was on the stage with the chief guest of the event and college management. Her parents and her husband with his son could see her sharing the stage with school dignitaries. This was her perfect gift for her father. She could see her father from the stage, that he was so happy and proud of her daughter. She could read his face and body language. He looked like, he was on the top of the world. The father looked very happy and felt proud of his daughter.

This was perfect moment from a daughter to a father. Father and daughter felt proud together with joyful tears in their eyes. Both Thanked almighty god for creating this moment for them and their family. Both felt indebted to god forever.

One of the teachers stood and said this moment was created for you and your father only, by god. Because you wanted to make your father happy and proud from the bottom of your heart. This was your selfless love and unconditional love for your father. You had a deep burning desire and you wanted it. Even though it was impossible at that moment in your life. God made it happen. Some people say miracles don't happen. But miracles do happen. Everyone in the classroom started clapping for the teacher Chandrika Jadhav.

After the session, I left that place. While coming back home I was thinking. "Miracles do happen."

I recalled the words of Paul Coelho from the novel "The Alchemist", "When you want something from the bottom of your heart, the entire universe conspires to achieve it."

Activity: Create a vision board that represents your goals and aspirations.

Chapter 5: The Miraculous Power of Belief

**The thing always happens that you believe in, and the belief in a thing makes it happen.
- Frank Lloyd Wright**

Belief is a powerful force that shapes our thoughts, actions, and ultimately, our reality. Whether we believe in ourselves, our dreams, or the world around us, our beliefs have the power to manifest in our lives in ways both subtle and profound.

At its core, belief is the acceptance that something is true or real, often without tangible evidence. This belief can be in ourselves, in others, or the universe at large. When we believe in something strongly enough, it has the power to influence our thoughts, emotions, and behaviours, leading us to take actions that align with our beliefs.

One of the most powerful aspects of belief is its ability to create self-fulfilling prophecies. When we believe in our abilities and potential, we are more likely to take risks, pursue our goals, and ultimately, achieve success. On the other hand, if we believe that we are incapable or unworthy, we are more likely to hold ourselves back and prevent ourselves from reaching our full potential.

Belief also plays a crucial role in how we perceive the world around us. Our beliefs shape our reality, influencing how we interpret events and interact with others. For example, someone who believes in the inherent goodness of people is more likely to trust others and form positive relationships, while someone who believes that people are inherently selfish may be more guarded and skeptical in their interactions.

The power of belief is perhaps most evident in the realm of healing. Studies have shown that patients who believe in the effectiveness of a treatment are more likely to experience positive outcomes, regardless of the actual efficacy of the treatment. This phenomenon, known as the placebo effect, highlights the profound impact that belief can have on our physical and mental well-being.

So how can we harness the miraculous power of belief in our own lives? The key is to cultivate beliefs that are positive, empowering, and aligned with our goals and values. This may require challenging limiting beliefs that no longer serve us and replacing them with new, more empowering beliefs.

One way to cultivate positive beliefs is through affirmations. By repeating positive statements about ourselves and our abilities, we can begin to shift our beliefs and thoughts in a more positive direction. Visualization can also be a powerful tool for reinforcing positive beliefs, as it allows us to mentally rehearse success and envision our goals coming to fruition.

Ultimately, the power of belief lies in our willingness to embrace it. By cultivating beliefs that empower us and align with our goals, we can harness this power to create the life we desire and manifest our dreams into reality.

We only see what we want to see; we only hear what we want to hear. Our belief system is just like a mirror that only shows us what we believe. Don Miguel Ruiz

One day a young man came to enquiry about communication skills development. I was in the cabin and busy. He entered my cabin. He introduced himself as Santosh Borade. He started complaining about the tantrums of the new-aged girls. He started in an annoying and angry voice, "Sir, looking for girls for marriage. I had met many girls. Many girls are rejecting me, by saying that I can't speak good in English. They don't want to get married to me. I am tired of these girls and their tantrums. Some say, "I am a commerce graduate and they want to get married, only engineers or doctors." Some say, "You earn only Rs. 32,000/- per month. I want to marry a gay who earns a minimum of Rs. 50,000/- or more per month." Some say, "You have only a 1BHK flat in Mumbai. That is not enough. A family must have at least 2 BHK flats." Some say, "I don't want to live in a joint family. I would like to live in a nuclear family only and you have a mother." I don't know whether I would get a suitable bride for me. I have left the hope of getting married now. I was listening to this patiently.

After finishing his words, I asked him about his problems, his level, requirements, and his expectations from me and the institute. I gave all the details about the course and fees details. After listening to all the details, Santosh paid the fees and joined the course.

He was present for 2nd day session. During the session, he received a call on his phone and asked my permission to receive the call. He had a long conversation outside the classroom for around 15 – 20 minutes. Then he had resumed the session. After 2nd day's session, he came to me and requested that, he had received a call from a father of a girl during the session and he would be going to meet him next day. So he would not be able to attend the next session.

I received a call from Santosh after one month of his session of 2nd day. He would not be able to attend the session for another month. Because he would be getting engaged within a couple of weeks he had to do a lot of preparation. So I said, alright, by the way, congratulations Santosh on your engagement. He gladly said, "Thank you, Sir."

After this incident, he again called me, Sir, I cannot attend the sessions for another 1-2 months I am getting married soon. I wished him, "Good luck Santosh."

After 6-7 months he appeared in the branch office with a sweet box in his hand. He attended the session on that day. End of the session he distributed all the sweets to all his classmates. He then started sharing his experience in the Maxam Mind and with me. This place has some magic. It is mysterious to me. This place is lucky for me. I came to this place in frustration. I had lost my hope of getting married. Sir listened to me patiently and he made me comfortable. He consoled me. The day came with disappointment here my good days started coming my way. He thanked me and this place Maxam Mind. He left the place in gratitude.

Activity: Meditate for 10 minutes daily, focusing on a personal belief or positive thought.

Chapter 6: Synchronicity and Serendipity

"We do not create our destiny; we participate in its unfolding. Synchronicity works as a catalyst toward the working out of that destiny." - David Richo

Synchronicity and serendipity are two mystical concepts that often leave us in awe of the mysterious ways in which the universe unfolds. They remind us that there is more to life than meets the eye and that sometimes, the most extraordinary events can occur when we least expect them. At the heart of these phenomena lies the power of positive thinking and an attitude of gratitude, which can act as catalysts for attracting meaningful coincidences and fortuitous encounters into our lives.

Understanding Synchronicity and Serendipity: Synchronicity, as coined by Carl Jung, refers to meaningful coincidences that occur without any discernible causal connection. These events often carry a profound message or significance that resonates with our innermost being. Serendipity, on the other hand, refers to the occurrence of events by chance happily or beneficially, leading to unexpected and fortuitous outcomes.

The Role of Positive Thinking: Positive thinking is a mindset that focuses on the bright side of life, expecting favourable results and believing in one's ability to overcome challenges. This optimistic outlook can create a fertile ground for synchronicity and serendipity to flourish. When we maintain a positive attitude, we are more likely to notice and appreciate the subtle signs and opportunities that the universe presents to us.

For example, imagine someone who is searching for a new job. With a positive mindset, they approach each job application with enthusiasm and confidence, believing that the right opportunity will come their way. In doing so, they may come across a job listing that aligns perfectly with their skills and interests, leading to a serendipitous job offer that changes their life for the better.

The Role of Gratitude: Gratitude is the practice of acknowledging and appreciating the good things in life, no matter how small. It is a powerful force that can shift our focus from what we lack to what we have, opening our hearts to the abundance that surrounds us. When we cultivate an attitude of gratitude, we are more attuned to the blessings and gifts that come our way, including synchronicities and serendipitous events.

Positive thinking and an attitude of gratitude are powerful tools that can enhance our experience of synchronicity and serendipity. By cultivating these qualities, we can open ourselves up to the magic and mystery of life, allowing us to embrace the unexpected and welcome the extraordinary into our lives. As we continue on our journey, let us remember that the universe is always conspiring in our favour and that the dance of destiny is guided by the light of our positive thoughts and grateful hearts.

"Synchronicity occurs at the intersection of your awareness, response, perspective, and action."
— Andrea Goeglein

Aarti Mehta joined Maxam Mind to improve her English communication skills and personality. She was living in the next building of our Kharghar branch. She was living with her husband in a nuclear family. Her husband was a Chartered Account and working for ONGC public sector.

Aarti had been suffering from asthma since her childhood. She was not keeping well sometimes. She was on medication. But she was attending most of the classes sincerely. She was kind too. She gifted me a pot to keep water for pigeons in my building. She told me Sir, birds don't get enough water to drink in hot summer so most of the birds die due to unavailability of water. She insisted I serve water to the pigeons in the summer. I still have that pot. Mostly in summer, I serve water to the pigeons and I always recall her whenever I see it.

Sometimes she would prepare nice Gujarati snacks and serve to the entire class including me. And a couple of times she bought samosas for everyone in the class. We all enjoyed her snacks.

During this course, she went to her hometown for her sister's engagement. One day,I got a call from her native place. Aarti said, "Sir, there is some good news." I asked her, "What is that?" She said, "I am pregnant." "Congratulations Aarti" That's great news. And she continued, "You know sir, We have been planning to have kids, but I could not conceive for a long time. I was on medication for that. My doctor was very much surprised. 'How is it possible?' I told my doctor, I am attending a personality development course. The environment of the class is very positive and pleasing. I am very happy and love attending these sessions. I have a good time learning and spending time with my teacher and my classmates. That may be the reason." I was completely surprised to hear this. It is unbelievable. If I tell this to anyone people may call me mad. No science can prove this, that just the practice of gratitude, meditation, and pranayama can do so many miracles. If somebody tells me this, I may not believe this but this is the fact. It just happened in front of my eyes. Sometimes truth is stranger than fiction.

Activity: Keep a synchronicity journal for a month, noting any meaningful coincidences that occur.

Chapter 7: The Protective Shield of Gratitude: How Positive Thinking Can Keep You Safe

"Once you replace negative thoughts with positive ones, you'll start having positive results." – Willie Nelson

In a world filled with uncertainty and challenges, it can be comforting to believe that positive thinking and gratitude can act as a protective shield against misfortune. While this idea may seem wishful thinking or superstition to some, there are many scientific evidences to support the notion that our mindset and emotions can have a profound impact on our physical and mental well-being. In this chapter, will explore the scientific basis behind the idea that positive thinking and gratitude can help keep us safe, and how we can cultivate these qualities in our own lives.

Positive thinking is more than just a happy-go-lucky attitude; it has real, measurable effects on our brains and bodies. When we think positively, our brains release chemicals called endorphins, which are natural painkillers and mood elevators. These endorphins not only make us feel good, but they also help reduce stress and anxiety, which can have a positive impact on our overall health.

Studies have also shown that positive thinking can boost our immune system. When we think positively, our bodies produce more white blood cells, which are responsible for fighting off infections and diseases. This means that positive thinking can help us stay healthier and more resilient against illness.

Gratitude is closely related to positive thinking, and it too has been shown to have a powerful impact on our well-being. When we feel grateful, our brains release dopamine and serotonin, which are neurotransmitters associated with pleasure and happiness. These chemicals not only make us feel good in the moment, but they also help improve our overall mood and outlook on life.

In addition to its effects on our brain chemistry, gratitude has also been linked to better physical health. Studies have shown that people who practice gratitude regularly have lower blood pressure, improved heart health, and stronger immune systems. Gratitude has also been shown to reduce symptoms of depression and anxiety, making it a powerful tool for improving mental health.

So how exactly do positive thinking and gratitude help keep us safe? These practices help us maintain a more optimistic outlook, which can help us better cope with stress and adversity. When we face challenges with a positive attitude, we are more likely to find constructive solutions and less likely to succumb to negative emotions like fear and anxiety.

Positive thinking and gratitude can also help us build stronger social connections, which are essential for our well-being. When we express gratitude towards others, we strengthen our relationships and build a support network that can help us in times of need. This sense of connection and belonging can provide us with a sense of security and safety, knowing that we are not alone in facing life's challenges.

Another way that positive thinking and gratitude can keep us safe is by helping us make better decisions. When we approach situations with a positive mindset, we are more likely to see the potential risks and benefits clearly, allowing us to make informed choices that prioritize our safety and well-being.

Positive thinking and gratitude are not just feel-good concepts; they are powerful tools that can help keep us safe and resilient in the face of life's challenges. By cultivating these qualities in our own lives, we can build a protective shield that helps us navigate the ups and downs of life with grace and confidence. So, the next time you find yourself facing adversity, remember the power of positive thinking and gratitude and let them guide you towards a brighter, safer future.

"There are only two ways to live your life. One is as though nothing is a miracle. The other is as though everything is a miracle." – Albert Einstein

One fine morning in 2021 I got a call from the office building my neighbour Mr. Kiran Kumar from the same floor. We both had our offices on the 4th floor by saying that Burglars entered your office last night and please come and check. My unit number is 406 and Kiran Kumar's unit number is 403.

Immediately I rushed to the office. I unlocked the door and entered the office. I checked the entire office unit. Everything was as it was. There was no movement of anything in the office. Everything was found to be as there were. There was no suspicious movement. Everything was perfect as it was. Touch wood nothing happened. I was so grateful.

But the story of our office building was not the same. It was different. Burglars came last night on our floor. They tried to break office number 403 through the main door. Tried hard but couldn't get in. They tried to break the main door of 404. They could not enter through the main door. They entered 404 through the washroom window. They entered and stole cash from 404. They entered 405, and they moved the entire office but did not steal anything from 405. They entered office number 407 through the washroom window by overpassing 406 my office. They stole a lot of cash from 407 the same night.

Floor plan

		407	Staircase	Lift
	406	Passage		
		405	404	403	402

Building passage person can walk the entire building

After a lot of thinking and analysis, I have the conclusion that with the continuous and consistent practice of gratitude, meditation, and pranayama, we not only get what we want, and manifest our wishes, desires, and dreams we are protected against any bad luck or negativity. This is the invisible power that surrounds us wherever we live or where we go. This was not less than any miracle. Touchwood I was saved from a misfortune.

Activity: Write a letter to your future self, outlining your hopes and the changes you wish to embrace.

Chapter 8: From Despair to Hope: A Journey of Recovery

"Instead of worrying about what you cannot control, shift your energy to what you can create."
— Roy T. Bennett

Life's challenges can often leave us feeling overwhelmed and defeated, especially when faced with adversity and despair. However, amidst the darkest of times, there lies a beacon of hope and resilience that can lead us from despair to a path of recovery and growth. This journey is not easy, but with the power of positive thinking and an attitude of gratitude, it becomes a transformative experience.

Positive thinking is more than just a mindset; it's a powerful tool that can change the way we perceive and respond to challenges. When faced with difficulties, those who embrace positive thinking are more likely to see setbacks as temporary and solvable. They focus on solutions rather than problems, which can lead to a more optimistic outlook on life.

An attitude of gratitude goes hand in hand with positive thinking. Gratitude allows us to shift our focus from what is lacking in our lives to what we already have. This shift in perspective can have a profound impact on our mental well-being, helping us to feel more content and hopeful, even in the face of adversity.

When we combine positive thinking with an attitude of gratitude, we create a powerful mindset that can help us overcome even the greatest of challenges. Instead of dwelling on the negatives, we learn to see the positives in every situation. This doesn't mean ignoring the difficulties we face; rather, it's about finding strength and resilience in the face of adversity.

One of the key benefits of positive thinking and gratitude is their ability to reduce stress and anxiety. By focusing on the positives in our lives, we can reduce the impact of negative emotions and cultivate a sense of calmness and peace. This can be particularly beneficial during times of recovery, when stress levels are often heightened.

Furthermore, positive thinking and gratitude can improve our overall outlook on life. When we approach challenges with a positive mindset, we are more likely to find creative solutions and opportunities for growth. This can lead to a greater sense of fulfillment and satisfaction in our lives, even in the midst of difficulties.

the journey from despair to hope is a challenging one, but it is not impossible. By embracing positive thinking and an attitude of gratitude, we can transform our outlook on life and find the strength to overcome even the greatest of challenges. So, the next time you find yourself facing adversity, remember the power of positivity and gratitude. They may just be the keys to unlocking a brighter, more hopeful future.

"Learn from stars; even in the dark they give off light, not despair."
— Matshona Dhliwayo

This year 2023, has shaken me completely. My mother was hospitalized, due to some blockage in the spinal cord. She was not able to stand, walk, and even eat with her own hands. I could not see her in that condition. The fear of losing her was unacceptable. Qualified and experienced neurosurgeons could not be treated even after surgery. All my family and relatives had accepted that we would be losing mother forever. For me, it was unacceptable and I was not ready for this.

This was like the end of the world for me. Dead end. I would lose my mother forever. I was crying as a small baby. I lost my thinking. I became mad. I broke emotionally and mentally completely.

Usually, I don't cry. No problem with money, or career, made me ever cry. I am emotionally and mentally strong and balanced. This time I was lost. I was overwhelmed.

May, June, and July months are the peak season of my business for me. I do the highest business out of the whole year. But during this, I was mostly traveling every weekend to my hometown. Due to this, I could not concentrate on my business. I lost the peak of the season of my business.

I heard saying that, misfortune never comes alone. It was my turn to face it. I don't know about salaried people, but businessmen or digital marketers understand the importance of Google My Business. It is a local Google page, and most of the local businesses are registered here. 90% of my business and revenue comes through Google My Business only. Do you know what happened? My business contact number disappeared one fine day in July only. Due to this, I lost a major chunk of business in July, August, and September. It impacted even October and November.

Once again I started practicing gratitude, meditation, and pranayama vigorously. I had a deep desire to somehow overcome the difficulties of my mother's health issues. I was expecting some miracle to happen in my life. Every day and every moment I was praying for her good health.

One day suddenly I called my sister Rangamma and asked about mother's health condition my sister told me Mother that, she was able to stand now and walk herself with the help of a walker. To be frank, I couldn't believe my ears what she said. I asked her to shoot a video and send it. Within minutes, she shared a video of her standing and walking with the support of a walker. Yes, she was able to stand on her own feet. My prayers were answered. Gradually she regained her strength to stand and walk. Nowadays she can walk without the support of a walker or a stick. I am so happy and grateful to the almighty that I could hear my voice. I can see in front of me. She is happy, healthy, and strong enough to stand and walk. Thank you. Thank you. I feel now, that I am blessed. I see all the wealth in her unconditional love. Recovering from such a critical situation is not a less than a miracle. This is all possible only because of spirituality.

The power of gratitude, pranayama, and meditation cannot be explained in words. It cannot be proven in science labs. No experiment can give the proof.

Today I feel blessed with the power of the magic of gratitude. Once we understand and realize the magical power of gratitude we can bring more magic into our life every day and every moment.

Activity: Engage in an act of self-care each day for a week, documenting how each activity made you feel.